Max
And his Big Imagination

✦ NEW ZEALAND ✦
ACTIVITY BOOK

by
Chrissy Metge

www.chrissymetge.com
www.ducklingpublishing.com

all about Me

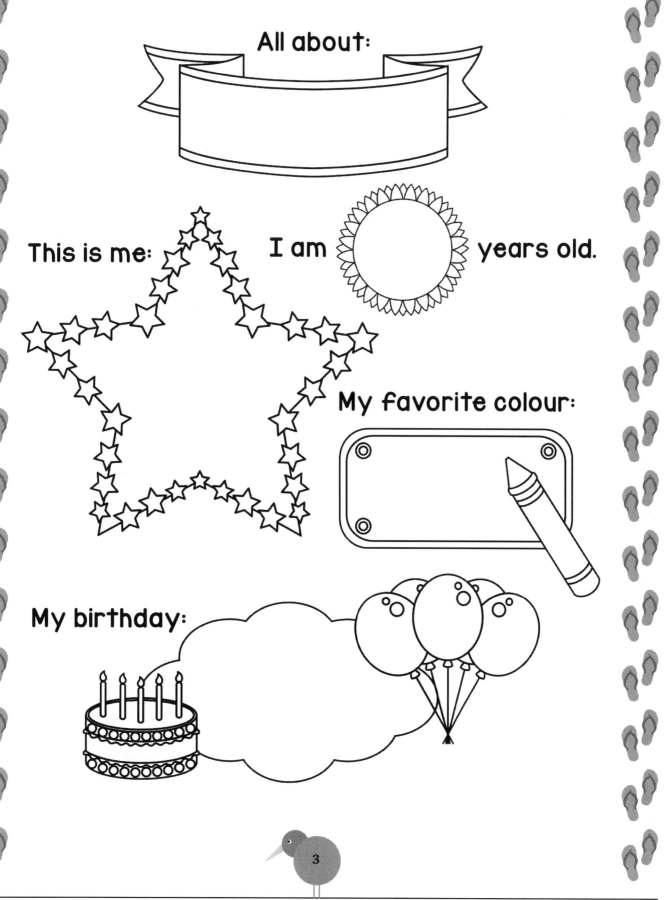

All about:

This is me:

I am _____ years old.

My favorite colour:

My birthday:

3

WARM UP WORK

Follow the lines.

4

DRAW IN THE SHAPES

Fill in the shapes with anything you want!

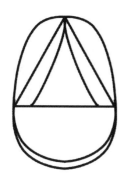  

 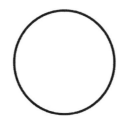 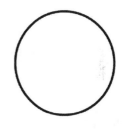

 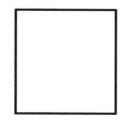 

5

DRAW IN THE SHAPES

Fill in the shapes with anything you want!

 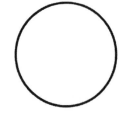 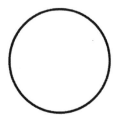

 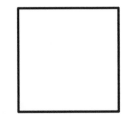 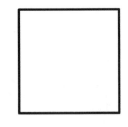

6

☆ COLOUR THE KIWI ☆

Use the colour key to colour the kiwi.

1 = yellow   2 = brown   3 = green

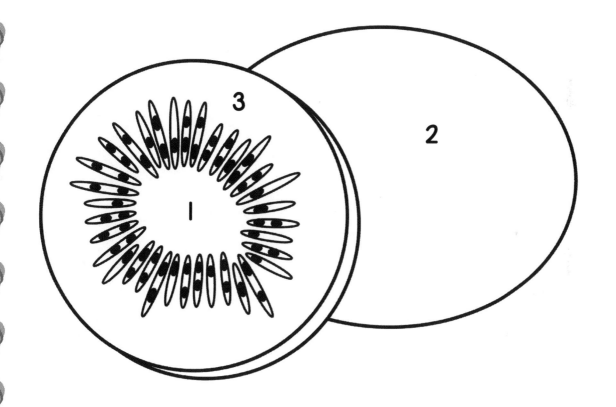

Max and his Big Imagination: New Zealand Activity Book

HOW TO DRAW

Learn how to draw jandals!

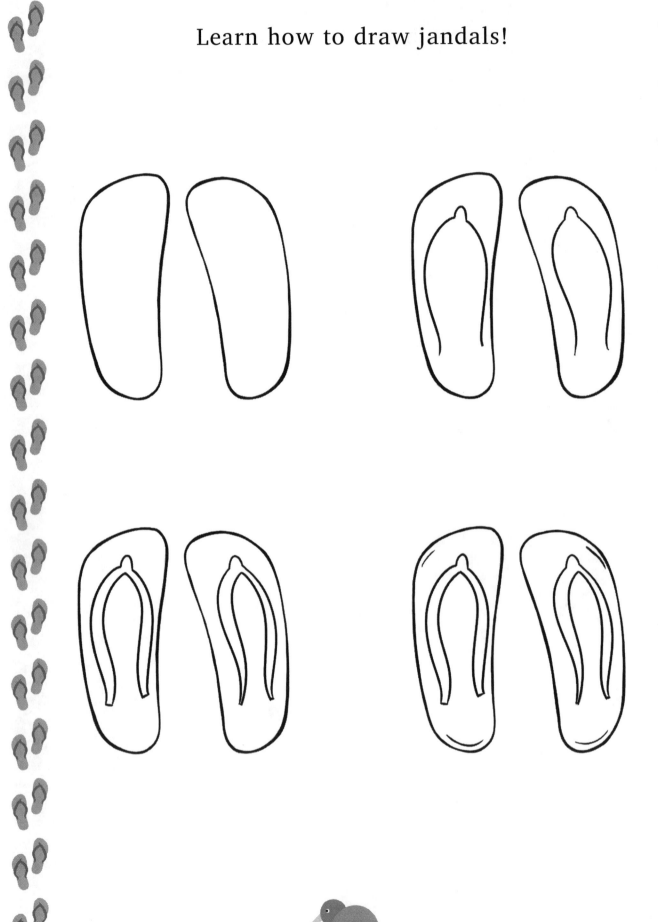

Max and his Big Imagination: New Zealand Activity Book

⭐ HOW TO DRAW ⭐

Draw your jandals here.

9

Find the path through the maze.

10

Finish the Weta.

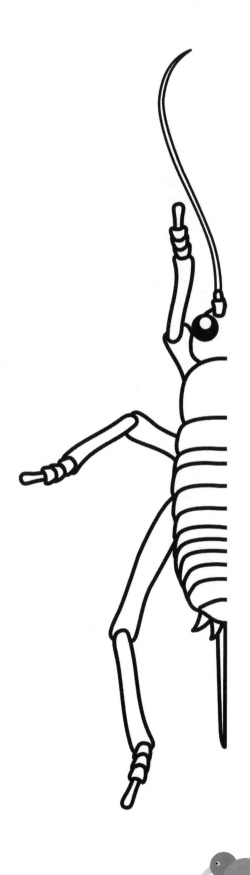

11

COUNT AND WRITE

Count and colour the NZ icons. Record the number!

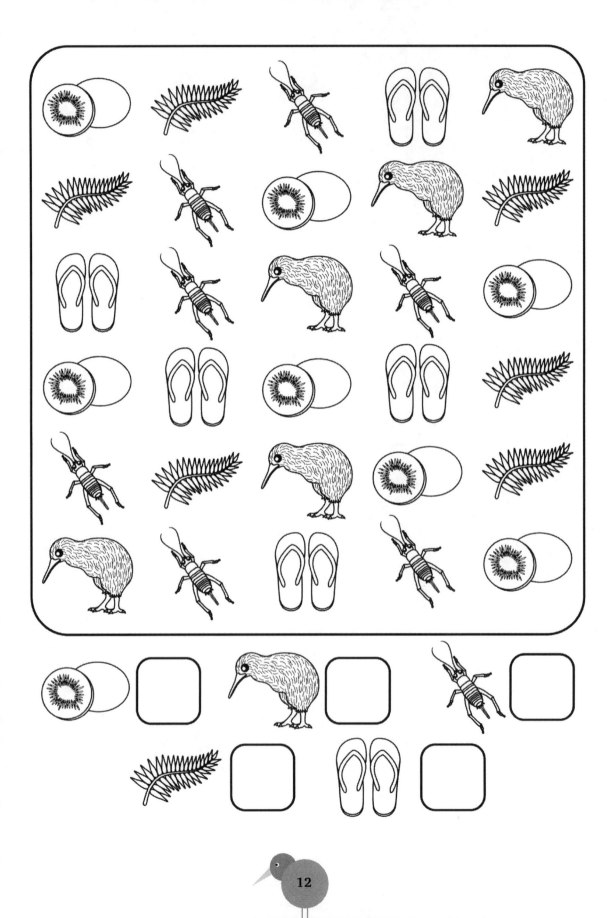

COLOUR THE PICTURE

Design your own New Zealand map!

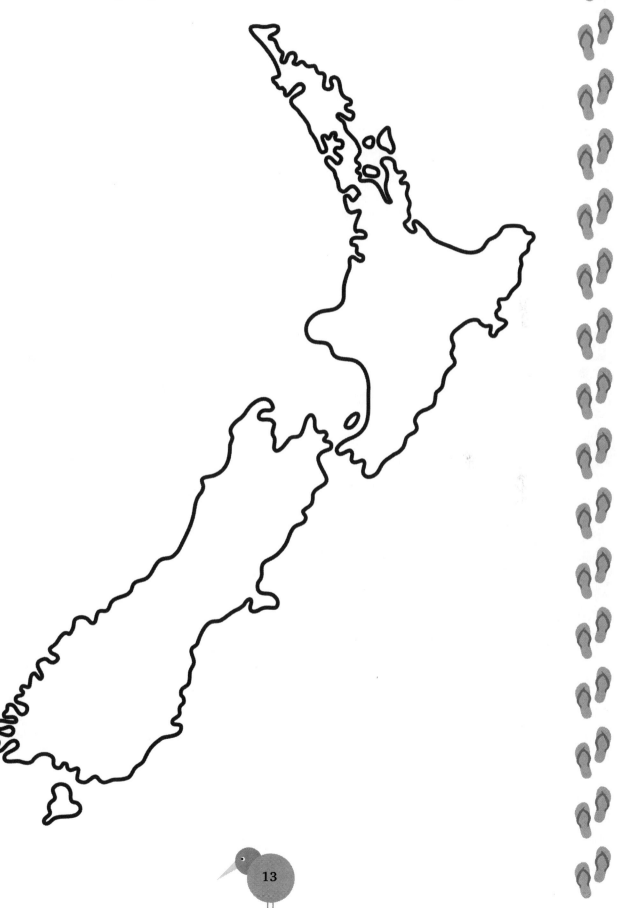

Max and his Big Imagination: New Zealand Activity Book

HOW TO DRAW

Learn how to draw the map of New Zealand!

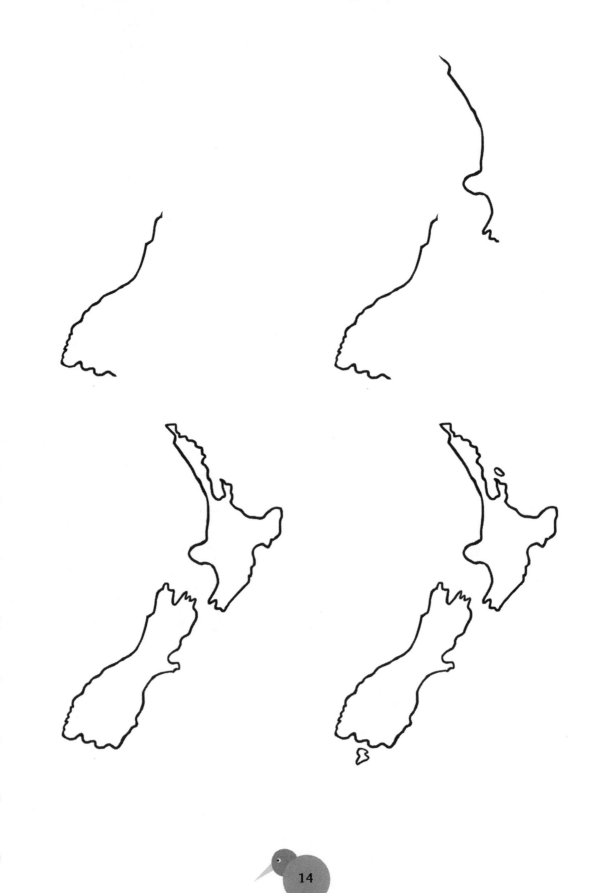

HOW TO DRAW

Draw New Zealand here.

15

COLOUR THE PICTURE

Colour the flag!

16

CONNECT THE DOTS

Connect the dots of the New Zealand Fern.

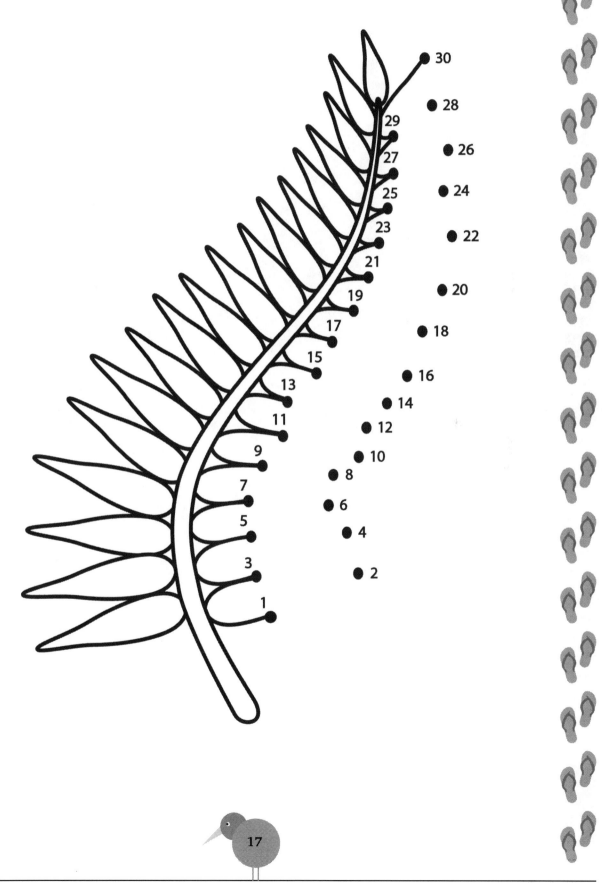

Max and his Big Imagination: New Zealand Activity Book

Finish the Pukeko!

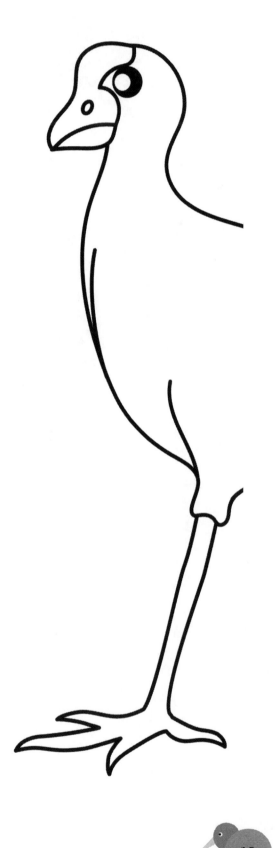

FIND THE PATH

Find the path through the maze.

COLOUR THE PENGUIN

Use the colour key to colour the penguin.
Can you guess what New Zealand penguin this is?

1 = yellow   3 = blue   5 = green

2 = orange   4 = grey

Max and his Big Imagination: New Zealand Activity Book

MATCHING GAME

Draw a line to the matching shadow.

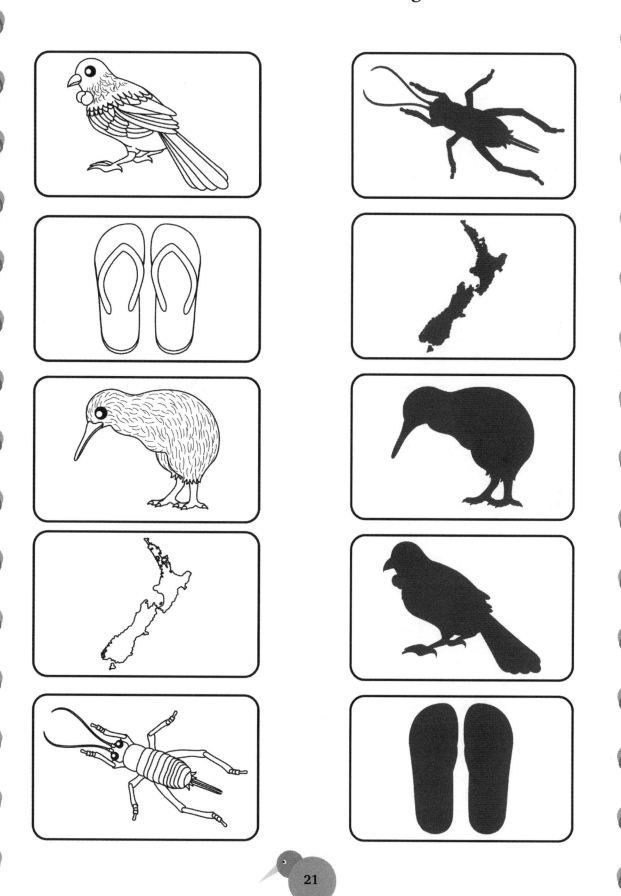

Max and his Big Imagination: New Zealand Activity Book

☆ COUNT AND WRITE ☆

Count the animals and write the number below!

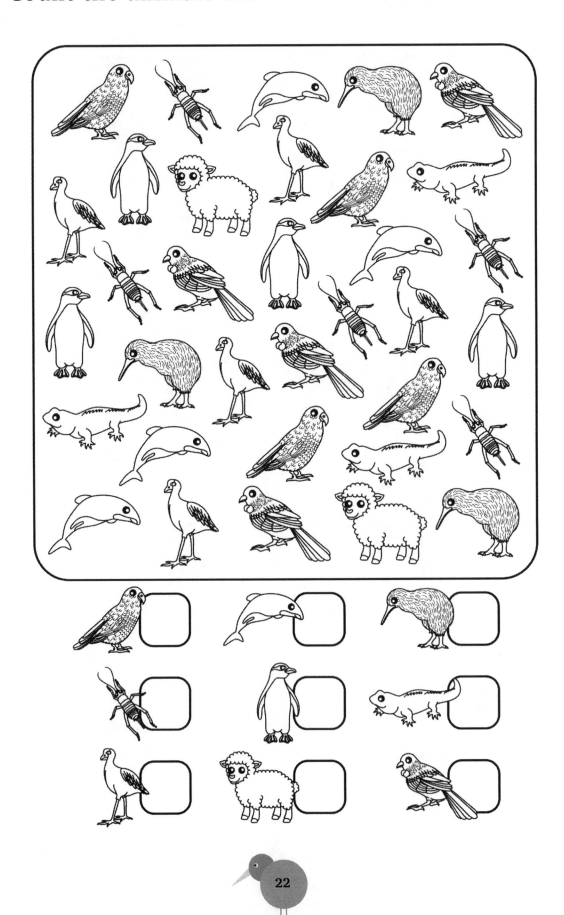

COLOUR A PICTURE

Trace and colour this Koru Fern.

23

CONNECT THE DOTS

Connect the dots of the Maui Dolphin from A to Z.

TRACE THE NUMBERS

Trace the numbers 1 to 10.

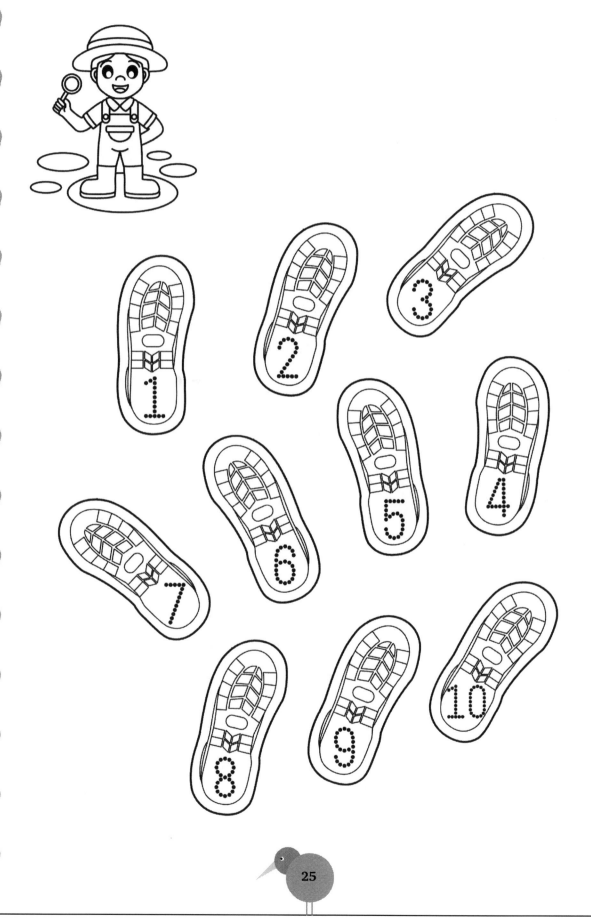

Max and his Big Imagination: New Zealand Activity Book

 HOW TO DRAW

Learn how to draw a kiwi!

26

HOW TO DRAW

Draw your kiwi here.

27

TRACE THE LETTERS

Trace the letters A to Z.

a b c d

e f g h

i j k l

m n o p

q r s t

u v w x

y z

Max and his Big Imagination: New Zealand Activity Book

MYSTERY PUZZLE

Cut along the lines and put the puzzle together.
Can you guess what New Zealand bird this is?

⭐ MASK ⭐

Colour and cut out your Kaka bird mask!

WHAT COMES NEXT?

Cut out and find the matching picture.

   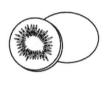 

Max and his Big Imagination: New Zealand Activity Book

Design your own Jandals and cut them out!

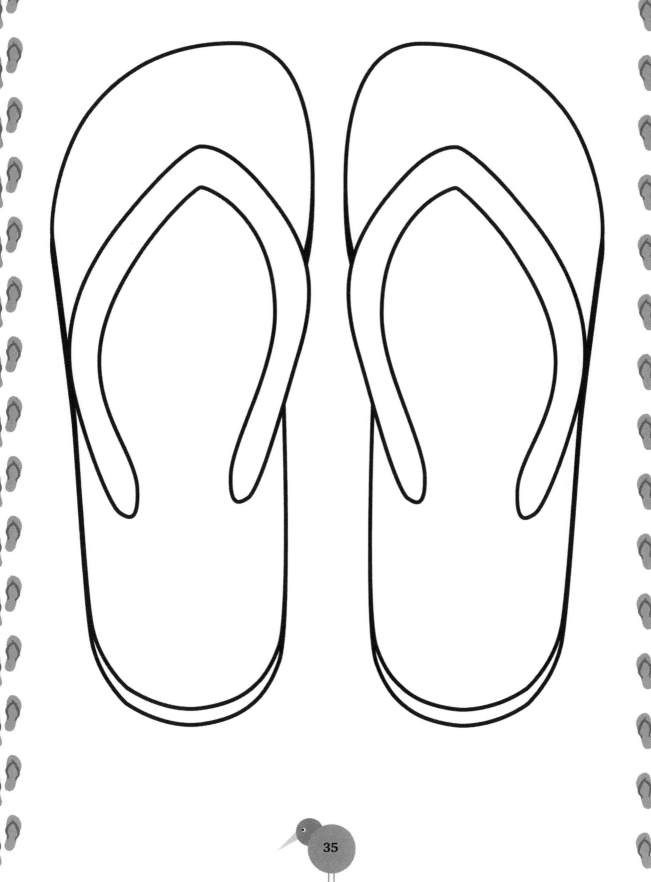

35

Max
And his Big Imagination

Check out our other activity books!

Transport Activity Book   Seaside Activity Book
Space Activity Book   Safari Activity Book
Dinosaur Activity Book   Castle Knight Activity Book

Read, Play, Imagine!

www.ducklingpublishing.com